New Voices

New Voices

Selected by Lorna Goodison

Poet Laureate of Jamaica 2017–2020

The University of the West Indies Press
Jamaica • Barbados • Trinidad and Tobago

NATIONAL LIBRARY OF JAMAICA

The University of the West Indies Press
7A Gibraltar Hall Road, Mona
Kingston 7, Jamaica
www.uwipress.com

The National Library of Jamaica
12 East Street
Kingston, Jamaica
nlj.gov.jm

A catalogue record of this book is available from the National Library of Jamaica.

ISBN: 978-976-640-785-8 (paper)
978-976-640-786-5 (Kindle)
978-976-640-797-2 (ePub)

Cover illustration: Lorna Goodison, untitled.
Book design by Robert Harris
Cover design by Abigail Henry
Set in Dante 11/15

Printed in the United States of America

CONTENTS

PART II

PART III

FOREWORD

This anthology is an exemplary product of Lorna Goodison's promotion of Jamaican poetry during her tenure as poet laureate. Her workshops for young people, held across the island, have proven highly successful. Particularly innovative have been the workshops under the caption "All Flowers Are Roses: Poetry and Self-Defence". This series, beginning with a focus on girls, responded soon enough to a need to include boys, and it has enhanced in the process the addressing of gender-based violence and the awareness of the value of poetry in this regard.

Beyond the achievement of the workshops have been the prizes Goodison has instituted for young poets, beginning with the Helen Zell Young Writers' Prize for Poetry, a benefaction of the University of Michigan, Ann Arbor, where she was professor in the Department of African-American Studies. She then instituted, funded by herself, prizes in the names of three Jamaican poets. This practical gesture will no doubt have evoked in the entrants for the prizes a sense of their taking their place in a tradition. The poems in this anthology are the prize-winning and other short-listed entries for the prizes.

The anthology impresses with the general maturity of the poetry, in respect of the engagement with ideas, the evocation of experience and the exercise of craft. The anthology is not to be relegated to the level of "just for young people". It takes its place, deservedly, as an addition to the widening world of Jamaican poetry. It is a signal contribution of the poet laureate to that world.

PROFESSOR EDWARD BAUGH, CD
Chairman
Poet Laureate of Jamaica Committee

MESSAGE FROM THE HELEN ZELL WRITERS' PROGRAM

When asked if the Helen Zell Writers' Program (HZWP) at the University of Michigan would be willing to partner with the Poet Laureate of Jamaica Committee in honouring Lorna Goodison by contributing to a poetry prize in her name for young poets, it was a collective no-brainer for the programme. Lorna served many years on faculty at the University of Michigan, teaching in the Department of English and for the HZWP's MFA programme, and her retirement left an absence that will never – indeed, could never – be filled. She was an invaluable member of this community, and we miss not only her wisdom but also her good spirit.

Personally, when I was first hired at the University of Michigan, I must admit that I was intimidated by Lorna. I had been reading her poems for years, studying her voice and her craft, and she was one of the icons I looked to as a benchmark both on the page and in how a person of colour could navigate academia while maintaining the integrity of one's voice. As a result, I found myself at a loss of words whenever I found myself in her presence. In my mind, I thought, "Why is Lorna Goodison making her own copies for class? Why is she on this committee with me? Isn't it enough that she's here, walking among us?" But after spending more time around her, what I learned was that her accomplishments and her publications had not changed her. Not that I knew her before, mind you, but it was clear that the woman I bumped into in the copy room and with whom I worked on committees had retained some part of herself that academia had not ruined. The magnanimous nature and sisterly spirit I experienced working with her was something that had to come from her training at home, as a child, in Jamaica – not from being the renowned figure I had been reading for years. The grace she exhibited daily at work was another lesson I learned from her, even now in middle age.

When asked to partner on a poetry prize that honours the work of young poets in Jamaica, the first thought that came to mind was that among these young writers, coming from the homeland of Lorna Goodison, there may be a generation of bright, intellectually curious minds with the same values and training that created this great woman. At the HZWP, we wanted to encourage as many of these young writers as possible. It has been an honour to partner with the poet laureate of Jamaica and to play a small role in supporting these young poets. It has also been an honour, once again, to connect the HZWP to the work, not simply on the page but also in the world, of Lorna Goodison.

AARON VAN JORDAN
Robert Hayden Collegiate Professor
Director, Helen Zell Writers' Program
The University of Michigan

JUDGING POEMS FOR THE EDWARD BAUGH PRIZE

It was a pleasure to read poems in consideration for the Edward Baugh Prize. Because I have enormous respect and great affection for both Edward Baugh and Lorna Goodison, it was all the more delightful. The mix of different kinds of poems was revelatory. So that I won't be suspected of sugarcoating, I admit upfront that some efforts were less successful than others. These poems might strive to remedy an injustice or give voice to a high moral sentiment or express a personal anguish or affection, but they hadn't yet found a way to move beyond generalities and well-worn phrases – the kind of undistinctive language that we tend to think in and to hear around us every day. But these attempts helped to make the stronger poems stand out all the more as wonders of creativity – fresh, vivid and energetic, each displaying distinctive strengths. As I turned from one file of poems to another, I felt as if I were stepping from one psychic and sensory world into another. The variety of subject matter was impressive. There were historical poems set in the moment of Columbus's fateful journey to the Americas or the vicious brutality and torture of slavery in the West Indies. Albeit public poems, they took an imaginative journey into the past and assumed the voice and perspective of another era. But there were also highly personal poems set in the present, dealing with love, sex, marriage, elation, grief, anger, loss and poverty. Some were narrative poems that offered a coherent story about falling in love or enduring a crime or cooking a soup, all compressed into a few lines. But there were also poems that in their lyricism stood outside narrative time and offered a glimmering moment. Some were written entirely in Jamaican Creole, some in standard English, and some nimbly switched between the two. Some were straightforward and delivered their sensory image with a punch; others were complicated puzzles, assembled in an intricate and unpredictable syntax. Some were especially well crafted in their music, rhythmically propelling the verse forward in vigorous cadences. Others were distinctive primarily because of their striking visual images. Some were expansive and open; others were gnarled inward, tightly compressed, spare. Some focused attention through their use of the line; others by the shape of the stanza. To read works by such a talented young group of emerging writers gave me hope for the future of poetry. I look forward to seeing what luminous and distinctive new worlds they will create for us in the coming years.

JAHAN RAMAZANI
University Professor and Edgar F. Shannon Professor of English
University of Virginia

THE POET LAURATE OF JAMAICA PROGRAMME AT THE NATIONAL LIBRARY OF JAMAICA

The National Library of Jamaica has had the privilege of being the administrator of the Poet Laureate of Jamaica programme since 2014. *New Voices* is a selection of poems by emerging young voices of Jamaican heritage and it is a fitting conclusion to the tenure of Lorna Goodison, the first woman to bear the title of poet laureate of Jamaica.

Goodison has demonstrated an unquestionable commitment to her role. Following her investment in May 2017, she launched an active tenure focusing on Jamaican youth and connecting them to an international creative network through the Helen Zell Writers' Program at the University of Michigan and other partners. We are therefore proud to introduce these poets on the recommendation of such venerable figures of the literary world. Maybe one of these poets will become the poet laureate of Jamaica someday.

The National Library of Jamaica extends its deepest gratitude to Lorna Goodison. She continues to be an outstanding champion for Jamaica's literary heritage and has cemented her place as a significant figure in contemporary world literature, having won numerous honours including the Commonwealth Poetry Prize and, recently, the Queen's Gold Medal for Poetry.

We thank the members of the Board of Management, the Poet Laureate of Jamaica Committee, and our parent ministry, the Ministry of Culture, Gender, Entertainment and Sport, for their ongoing support.

Thanks to the Jamaica Copyright Licensing Agency (JAMCOPY) and the Tourism Enhancement Fund for funding support of the programme. Special thanks are due to the Gleaner Company (Media) Limited, particularly Amitabh Sharma, for publishing the *Out of Many, One Poetry* series in the *Sunday Gleaner.*

Gratitude is expressed to the University of the West Indies Press for their careful handling of this publication.

BEVERLEY LASHLEY
National Librarian

INTRODUCTION

It is with great joy that I welcome the publication of this anthology featuring the winners of the Poet Laureate of Jamaica Prizes for Poetry, 2017–2020. The prizes for poetry were conceived out of my desire to encourage Jamaica's young poets, to offer them some monetary reward – because poetry is not normally a money-making concern – and a chance to have their work read and appraised by one of the top MFA programmes in the world.

We launched in 2017 with one prize sponsored by the Helen Zell Writers' Program at the University of Michigan, where I was fortunate enough to teach for over twenty years. But the considerable number of entries received in the first year made it clear to me that there were simply too many gifted Jamaican poets who were producing strong work for there to be just one prize. So, my husband Ted Chamberlin stepped forward and provided the money for a second winner, and we awarded two prizes in March 2018.

Later that year, I was blessed to win the Windham-Campbell Prize for poetry from Yale University, and that allowed us to add to the complement of prizes at the same time that we extended our partnerships to include the University of Virginia's prestigious Center for Poetry and Poetics. The three additional prizes created have been named for Jamaicans who have made stellar contributions to the world of English literature, locally and internationally: Edward Baugh, pre-eminent literary critic and poet; the late literary critic and poet Michael Cooke, a son of Jamaica who became the first black professor in the Department of English at Yale University; and Louise Bennett-Coverley, who is the very personification of Jamaican poetry.

The poems in this gathering introduce us to the works of writers at various stages of development, hailing from a variety of literary backgrounds. All are talented poets. All bring something new and fresh and surprising to the Jamaican literary landscape. These poems speak to the ways in which we love and work, live and die; how we lament and how we praise. They speak to the past and prophesy the future. Many of them speak hard truths as they address social injustice, even as they celebrate what is best in us. All of them are well worth reading.

I express thanks to the National Library of Jamaica, for this unique opportunity.

I owe a great debt of gratitude to Abigail Henry, director of special programmes at the National Library of Jamaica, for the truly outstanding work she does for the Poet Laureate of Jamaica programme. Thank you, Abi!

I cannot thank Ted Chamberlin enough for the countless ways in which he has supported me in this poet laureate adventure.

To the judges: Professor Mervyn Morris, Professor Edward Baugh, Dr Anthea Morrison, Dr Michael Bucknor, Dr Isis Semaj-Hall, Dr Norval Edwards, Millicent Graham and Yashika Graham, who have all worked hard over these past three years to select our winners. Big thanks.

To Linda Gregerson, Doug Trevor, Van Jordan, and the MFA students at the Helen Zell Writers' Program at University of Michigan, sincerest thanks.

To Professor Jahan Ramazani and the Center for Poetry and Poetics, University of Virginia, heartfelt thanks.

To W.W. Norton for generous donations of copies of the *Norton Anthology of Modern and Contemporary Poetry* as gifts to our young poets, thank you.

LORNA GOODISON, CD
Poet Laureate of Jamaica 2017–2020

PART I

Khadijah Chin

LET IT ALL HANG OUT

She asks me why Jamaicans rake their yards every morning,
wonders why the lady next door
would rake up twice before noon!

I listen as she insists
that the leaves belong to the earth
and we should leave them to nourish the place of their birth
and soon, I am assaulted with
the odour of words
like "inorganic" and "biodegradable"

And it occurred to me to say to her:
Darling, here in the tropics,
we don't leave things out to hang
the way you "hang out"
and "hang ten".

Here, di most we hang out is clothes
but not fi too long
or else yuh neighbour will say
yuh careless
an sun will bun dem out
an dem will ketch bad colour

an my granny woulda cry shame a di way
yuh lef yuh bed dis mawnin
cause yuh mus always chant two psalms
an kneel fi journey mercy
just in case bad blessin' tek yuh

an yuh mus neva leave yuh bed unspread
for in case bad feeling hol yuh a road
an somebody affi carry yuh into yuh room,
at least yuh will cover yuh shame
an yuh mus wear good baggy go a road
for just the same purpose

an if my granny see how you wash your hair
an wear it wet come outta di house,
she woulda sen yuh right back inside.
Yuh nuh fraid yuh ketch fresh cold?

But to avoid all the rigmarole,
I smile and say,
"To each his own."

But no, my love, that's not how we do things here.
We cover what ground we can.

We rake up the leaves
while we watch the shame tree grow.

Jovanté Anderson

EASTER SUNDAY

after the last word
after the last *roboyoshatta*
after the incredible whiteness
of lilies and lace,
there is the breaking of bread.
here, i am the fish that you feed on,
embalmed in vinegar and thyme,
resting silent in this ceramic grave,
mouth agape, gasping as if i died
fighting, daring to claim Kingston
gutters, clad in garish greens and gold,
how my laugh-and-skin-out ruptures
the sacred, or else sashaying uptown
wrist limp, son of gentry, sipping rum,
and seasoned in the quietness of genteel
company. witness my brittle lives, how i
dare to breathe, even as murderous tongues
make a meal of me.

Lauren Delapenha

THE DARK ROOM

Tumorous, tumultuous it grew
in the bowels of a house without
a basement. Closet underneath the stairs –
I needed room without a view to grow
my photographs. It took a month to clear
the prison-cell-sized space
of mum's pre-cancer paraphernalia.
And then three weeks to run the stupid plumbing.
Another week of sprinkling salt to kill
the neat society of mould that blossomed
in the corner, like the Rorschach test
that stains my underwear once a month.

To see in darkness took no time at all.
My goal was simple: see with both eyes.
With one eye, I saw; the other dreamed.
The darkened eye develops in the dark
strange images, familiar as forgotten
memories. As I see my mother
sip her tea one orange afternoon,
I forget which eye is which, you see.

I spend an hour staring with both eyes at
the empty socket in the ceiling where
the bulb had burst right by my eye while I
was changing it, and after blinking once
I'd limped out, glass in feet and hand and eye,
and seen the stairs: limpid, lucid, splintered.
That was fifteen years ago today.
These are things that happened after that:

The doctor sighed and shrugged and didn't charge.
I broke all the mirrors in the house.
I did not cry. The cloud in my eye spread out
and calcified. I sold the couch and bought
a camera, not for any images,
but rather to stack the negatives
in the room beneath the stairs
that kept my mother's nineteen-sixties things.

I dream up a career, shooting
fashion models. I've long been drawn
to their exquisite symmetry, but also
to deformity – especially when self-imposed.
Their scapulae like angels' wings,
their collarbones like blades –
there's something beatific in the visible arrangement
of their skeletons. Imaginary
interviewers pose their euphemisms:
Do you take photos to compensate for . . . (pause)
I smile and blink as if to think and tell them,
Well, I don't take photos – only photographs.

None of that materialised, of course.
Today I lock the darkroom door from inside.
My negatives stay negative. I spread
them all out on the floor – what for?
Is it better not to see at all
than to long so much, so wantonly?
I close my eyes and try to see nothing.
Instead there is my mother, drinking tea.

Trevann Hamilton

RIO COBRE

She runs beside the road like a little girl
Peeking in and out of vegetation
Like a game of hide and seek
Giggling as she tumbles over rocks

When she upsets Mother
she is pelted with rain like punishment
Scolded by the heavens
She overtakes her restrictions
Tearing everything in her path
Roaring and screaming

Romardo Lyons

MY HOME – MY HELL ON EARTH

Orange and grey buildings, barren gardens,
Don't piss here; gratified above *renkess* spot.
Bullet holes paint the walls, rusty railings tremble.
Chipped, scratched, mismatched tiles.
No elevator. I see Miss Tin Tin, Derron, Audrey, Miss Dennis.
Good morning, Good evening, Good night.

Dogs bark when *Babylon* enter the zone.
Men still loyal to Dudus run through gully,
hide guns in the hole beside Wayne's cook shop.
Wayne sells weed from the one pot.
We see it, but we don't see it.
Informa fi dead.

My mother, brother, sister and I
on our bellies under the bed, beside an old suitcase.
Shoulder to shoulder, sweat to sweat.
Gunshots outside hitting high notes.
Electricity out, tanks on house tops bleeding, urine
held like faith, phones kept close waiting.
Waiting on my father.

All young men: metal on waist;
if he doesn't say *dawg* or bully the *fishy yute*, him a *fish*.
all girls: push on hospital beds; if she doesn't send nudes,
is a *hype gal*.

Romardo Lyons

19651

Saturday evening talk on the gully bank,
Beula's $250 fried chicken, white rice, curry gravy,
Orange juice from Beri's shop; rain drizzling,
not enough to send us running for shelter.
The jeep swings across the road,
as if steered by a drunk and I just know.
I know it's *green arm Dennis weh a look Keisha.*
His bald head wet, a dark face contoured with blackheads.
Back of his washed-out vest, 19651 in white bold.

He grips his AK-47, semi-automatic firm on belt.
I stare at his protruding left pocket,
wondering if it's weed, bloody kerchief, bullets,
a wrapped-up ratchet knife.
I wonder if his squaddies get annoyed;
the two that sit at the back of the jeep.
They sit waiting to see if Keisha will show up.

He shouts at us, points his baton,
His spit soar, into our circle.
kneel on the groun. shut your mout. respec authority.
He never arrests any of us. The same thing every week.
(he's just free entertainment)
He drags his feet back to the jeep,
crunching gravel. He opens the door,
wipes his head and neck with rag,
lifts his helmet from the front seat.
He puts it on, sits, starts the engine, speeds off.

Rohan Facey

BREAKING NEWS

Down Town bled like a slaughtered pig today,
Just like it did in recent times – legal guns
and illegal guns had
Guerrilla warfare,
and the children were in the way.

A regular morning – morphed into a scripted
scene from hell:
Stalls overturned.
Groceries spilled riotously.
Hole-riddled billboards gasped for breath;
and screams battered the air like frantic fists
against a closed door.

A starving artist (in a nearby corner),
Sprang to life, unfolded an easel
and began to daub the city – red, garish,
like the dancing flames of an inferno.

Flowers in the nearby park froze,
withheld their fragrance and listened with naked dread
to the chilling ricochet on the wind's airwaves – Death came to feast,
like vultures on a hapless village. Sorrowful sirens
wailed like bereaved Jamaican women.

And store shutters clanged and shivered into place,
unable to journey to normal hours

The radios started to twitter, like gossiping birds,
with breaking news –
for Down Town bled today.

TIEF LIKE PUSS

Puss stop slip through back door when yuh a cook,
an' climb through open window when yuh nah look.
Puss nuh haffi hide and loot.
Puss start wear three piece suit.
"Puss inna boot!"
Puss a host workshop, conference, seminar
Puss watch yuh tek bus
while Puss show up inna car.

Puss a get money weh lend.
Puss have big money a spend.
But Puss ongle gi' di contract to him fren dem.
So when $30 million road dig up back
fi put in $20 million pipe
Puss mek sure fi 'im ting line up right.

Puss a talk bout project fi implement,
Puss a talk bout national development.
Puss a draft policy weh nuh mek sense.
But true seh Puss a talk inna farrin accent,
everybody feel seh dis time it a go different.

Puss a consult but nuh know local context.
But Puss nuh care who vex
cah when dis done, Puss gwen collect
and just move on to di next.

A nuh just Puss weh tief!

Rhea Manley

GOLD FOR THE CHAINS

Before our flag was saltire set
we chose and signified colours –
Black for the hardships suffered by the people.
Green for the land, and hope for the future.
Gold for the sunshine and natural resources.

Bwoy . . .

the man who wrote that could
never have revised since independence:
gold for the chains drug lords don,
green for the harbour of algae, shit and cargo ship
and black? that's for the funerals, you hear.

But foreigner, look what you might find if you come:

gold, in the tan you may take from our sun
if you get out before you skin bun,

a shimmer of green as a doctor bird flits
out of your reach, can't catch his magic.

you might be bold, try Blue Mountain black,
or be basic, with a latte from Starbucks' tap.

But we, too, can
dip in the Blue Lagoon on a bright yellow sun day,
brave Black River crocs, to sample pepper janga
sport gold on our necks after races hard-won.

Sadé Young

COMMODORE DISTRICT

My street carries shades depending on where you look.
An icy blue lingers in the yard of my neighbour.
News gathers at our lips, rearranging stories like Chinese telephone.
They say her ex-lover, in a fit of rage, shot her son.
Some say in the leg but my brother says it's the heart.

The heart –
lilac hearts of the young congregate behind the shop at the junction.
They exchange kisses and hickeys, chasing the high of promised love
while old men in orange tones gamble and drink the night away.

Two houses down, Miss Morris is a mouth filled with kerosene,
her husband, the match.

On Sundays, we become mellow in this sun.
Gospel music echoes through the houses,
children knock apples off Mr Scott's tree
and the ice cream man passes by from time to time.

Peta-Gaye Williams

MY MOTHER'S TONGUE

My mother's tongue is a collection of languages
congregating in the mouths of this African
man, woman and child, a place where cultures meet
where history reminds us of where it has been.

This flavour of bended tongues, tells tales
of how our ancestors stripped bakkra massa's language
of it's grammar, inserted words from the motherland,
twisting a foreign tongue into submission.

An' dem seh our people neva revolutionary!
But dat is dyam well revolutionary to me
to have built a tongue of their own, borrowing words
from those who came, made our islands their home;
the Portuguese, English, Spanish, French, Asian, African.

Caribbean, formed from this blend of people
and cultures and tongues, with words like
afu, ackee, suo-so, nyam, deh go, de de, unu, yam
from the African languages that came on ships
with our people when our people were sold as slaves.

English is known to have one time been
Old Norse, Gaelic, German, Greek, French, Dutch,
Danish, Scots, Hebrew, Czech, Arabic, Welsh.
An' dem call fi wi language chaka-chaka
a corruption of the English language, a broken
substandard variety spoken by a variety of people
who are illegitimate, illiterate, a mere dialect.

But if you want to know the value of dis thing,
tell a Jamaican joke inna English ah yuh wi si wah mi a talk
see if di joke no lose its substance like it figet fi me yuh lauf.
Watch my granmada speak, hear her words shaking
An' moving, to di beat of reggae an' riddim an' drums.

My mother's mother's tongue, dem call it patwa,
I call it soul. They call it broken, I call it whole.

Rozan Levy

MICHI

Michi's mouth is a stall for Jamaican claat,
she sells to neighbours ears.
Voice drags before reaching the end of my name
as if carrying speaker boxes at her round robins
people barely attend.
What a way to use every partner draw she get.
She's the talk of my neighbourhood.
"Why she don't take the money do surgery,
get rid a di growt and stop mek noise a people head?"
But Michi big belly don't bother her
short and tight are her everyday clothes.
And if her belly hurt her, she come to my house,
tell mommy to pray and go testify how she heal.
Blink your eye, Michi hang claats inna the air again.
Michi loves to borrow, hates to repay
I know she memba wah ole bredda David say
the wicked borroweth and payeth not again.
Her light skin gets lighter, shows up its art,
colouring book not sold to children
but to men much older, and blasted Michi still owe me.

Delano Frankson

WALK WID YUH BASKET!

Lawks mah, a tell yuh seh mi bex!
A bex suh till a feel like mi heart deggo buss out a mi chest!

Miss Mavis seh she deggo run a boat,
Suh a seh: *alright, mi wi walk di journey guh dung town fi buy di things.*
Mi dear, after mi wash off mi foot and put on mi slippaz,
Hear the Miss Mavis she:
Suh tell mi something, is where yuh going without a basket?!
Mi have ova fifty basket in a house deh! Choose any one!
If mi neva in a mi clean clothes,
A wuda kick ova a grung and laugh.
Poor Miss Mavis!
Nuh know seh basket stop use and is lawda bag in style.
A haffi seh: *no Mavis, man. Shame on you. Yuh want town people laugh off a mi?!*
Dem nuh use basket no more. Mi goodly cya basket dung deh and dem call police fi lack mi up.
Mi dear child, a finally reach in a town
And a pick up the things in a di supermarket fi run fimmi and Mavis boat.
And afta di 'oman done cash di singting dem and a pay.
Mi realize she naa pack dem in a no lawda bag.
A seh: *but wait?! Is what yuh waiting on fi pack up mi things? Tip?!*
The woman start twist up har mouth and roll har yiy ball:
We don't have any scandal bag!
A was so shock! Mi poor likkle heart start tremble!
A lean and whisper to har: *'oman? How yuh mean fi seh yuh don't have any lawda bag?*

Mah, if a neva in a crowd,
Mi own a yiy wata would a ketch mi desso –
After mi never want a soul know wah mi buy.
Same time after di wud leff mi mouth,

Hear the 'oman shout out in a supermarket:
Excuse mi, sir . . . don't you hear I say wi don't have any scandal bag?!
NOW TAKE UP YUH SCRAPES MEAT AND YUH ONE POUN' A FLOUR
AND GET OUT!

A seh mah!
Mi tempa get di best a mi!
But a never want nobody fi know seh a country mi coming from,
Suh a put on a piece a haccent and a halla:
Rottewn teewth woman?! What you tarking 'bout scrapes meat?
Is my two pound a chicken bac' – a mean – chicken breast, yuh whanna
call scrapes meat?!

Di woman get bex!
Har nose open up like she out fi collapse.
She slam the counta and seh: *take up yuh things and leave di promises . . .*
yuh know yuh coming to shop, why yuh never walk wid yuh basket?!

Basket? A think to mi self.
A seh: *what you talking 'bout basket? Is country yuh grow?! Basket out a style!*

The 'oman pap a piece a laugh,
A almost think har denture would a drop out
Hear har: *after government ban lawda bag . . . basket back in style.*

A feel suh shame dat a never know seh govament ban lawda bag,
But yuh cyaa blame me . . .
Which part a country me fi tan from hear daa deh news?

Child, anyhow a did know seh lawda bag ban,
A would a walk wid Mavis fifty basket.
Just fi show di whole world seh mi up to the time.

Christopher Allen

BAUXITE TRAINS RED WITH RUST

I remember mama's house and the view from her verandah.
A large expanse of green; only interrupted by ripples of zinc roofs
and bauxite trains red with rust.

The furthest trees transform into blue sea.
A view that spans the Old Harbour Bay Power Station
and Rocky Point Alumina Port.

And I wonder why I haven't written about little girls counting ships,
smoke climbing the sky from a house on fire
and plagues of pigeon infesting the Hi-Pro Feed Factory.

Maas Frank's donkey, balancing burlap sacks of freshly burnt charcoal.
Trailers brake, belch and bend necks to contour Rasta Corner;
fearful of gullies swollen with drenched ghosts.

Sometimes my uncle stutters stories of a boy, barefoot and shirtless,
crying in midnight headlights.
Other nights he pours glass after glass of jokes while the ashtray fills.

Trevann Hamilton

EXPECTING

I carry the poems around in my belly
Pregnant and swollen
I don't forget the words are there
I can feel their weight under my heart.
I throw up the bitterness in the morning before I look at myself in the mirror

I can't write the poems until they are ready to be born
The day will come when I count the number times I gasp for air when I cry
My lungs contract and relax
That's when the pain comes in
And I reach for my pen and push
harder
And harder

Until I've birthed words on a lined page
Words that were growing deep inside me
Being nourished by me
I cradle all my troubles in beautiful stanzas

Gail Hoad

MIGRANT

Но вечно жалок мне изгнанник,
Как заключенный, как больной.
Темна твоя дорога, странник,
Полынью пахнет хлеб чужой.

I am not one of those who left the land . . .
Anna Akhmatova

Kingston's Palisadoes

Here at the tip of an extremity
Stretching out to sky and water
Salt air pinching wind and nose

Tenuous ties
pull taut here
stronger than ever.

Ever arcing north
glinting silver-white
clips wind-whipped
airstripped
kite-tailed
Flight.

A tug on the heart strings

A sting in the eye

This aching
never-ending
hollow-hurting
Goodbye.

| PART II |

Nardia Reid

TO MY GREAT-GRANDMOTHER

Everyone knows that you are starting to forget,
that no one steals your money,
that you hide it in places you can't remember,
and you don't tell us right when you find it.

We know you are too weak,
that arthritis makes it hard to build wood fire,
parch your chocolate seeds, pound them
then roll them with spice, ready to sell.

Now that you are deaf,
you wait until the middle of the night
to move from door to door to see if everyone is home,
if everyone is safe.

Before I fall asleep, I listen to you pray.
You beg God for your son to visit,
ask why he never comes even if you beg,
you send him sugar cane, yam, banana;
he never says thank you.

You ask God to kill you,
remind him your daughter is dead,
your friends are dead,
your spirit is dying.

Rojae Brown

PORTRAITS OF GRIEF

Funeral programmes in Jamaica are not only symbols of having been, they are symbols of nobility, marking off the called from the chosen. Returning from a funeral empty-handed is to have not gone at all.

Had I a programme, I would have left understanding.
Known what funeral home he was consigned to
or when the sun had shut on his one life.

I'd have seen his picture in grains and bundles
stamped, like a final passport to verify.
And say yes, that him was too black for true.

Finger the tributes and lessons of this family tree
second cousin after first cousin.
Even know to hush the common law who lay

brawlin claim to the once, incorruptible grief.
I'd have known the man who writhed against the casket
seams. Whispering the vacant words of the resurrection,

his last brother, the figure of his debt. I'd
have turned to its centre and traced the fractured
tableau of a life, lived in flashes. Maybe wonder

why all of the pictures are of Dainty and combolo,
hope to find one of him in corduroy, stoop down.
Fanning through the fulcrum of a life, how spent,
wondering mid-eulogy where he'd spend it next.
Hope to know the lineage of pallbearers who carry him
home. I'd have carried him home – with all the others.

Romardo Lyons

IT WAS MY FAULT

My pregnant stepmother Nora walks into the kitchen.
Right hand below her belly;
holding it like I would hang on to my swizzle and big foot
in the lunchroom at school.
She has my fish tank in her other hand.
Oval shaped, rainbow marbles, stones, one fish.
We'd clean it every two weeks.
Couldn't have Cherry swimming around in dirty water.
Nora's loose, yellow dress swaying left to right
because of her protruding belly.
The curtain flapping
in the breeze that made it through the crack.
When is your father going to patch that window?
Her swollen feet fit perfectly in my father's slippers.
She gives me the tank.
I open the lime green lid, smudging the glass,
my hand like a windscreen, wipes it smudge free.
I pour more than just water in the sink;
only marbles left in the tank.
Between smudging and un-smudging,
I forgot to take her out.
Dropped it; splinters still, marbles rolling around like pool balls.
Tried grabbing her, but it was as if I was moulding oil.
Cherry went round and round 'til the sink was lonely.
Nora turned off the pipe.

Christopher Allen

TEN YEARS LATER, I VISIT

Thirty yards behind the maze of concrete,
a shack backed by ply board flaking to dust.
Termites are drilling through the softened wood.
Rusty zinc door hangs by a bent nail.

Lizards changing colour, rotting Lignum vitae
limb leaning against the side; tired.
Wasp nest dangles from the collapsing roof.
A chorus of croaks and chirps echo
from knee high grass.

This shithouse was my father's
Sunday morning sanctuary. He read the *Gleaner*
sitting atop hollow, wooden, cube – inhaling deeply.
Him and the whole structure floated like flies.
The hole in the ground brimmed with stale news.

I keep his obituary, read it every Sunday morning
in the bathroom. The words are fading
like his face behind a cigarette, eyes red
as rust raining from the roof of a latrine.

Jovanté Anderson

VELVET

the best place for hide-and-seek
is in the closet.
when your cousin yells *readyornothereicome*
snicker into the velvet of your sister's
sunday best and listen for his footsteps in the distance.
no matter what, do not respond to his bellows,
to his temptations of gizzada cake or his giggle-ridden
warnings that granny coming next with the leather belt.
sit between the kitten heels, inhale the mothballs,
and think about how much you would like
to be a citizen of the closet, how this matchbox mecca
could be yours.
if you listen closely, you can hear the sound of feet
trampling shoes, fidgeting to fit into the everythingness
of this space, of sacred place, gleefully hiding, too.
you are never alone.
him don't ever need to find you
you don't ever need to come out

Delroy McGregor

THE BOY IN THE BEDROOM

I hope to pray away the moth
stained drapes, molding walls,
dirty windows, and stripping
black boots in the closet. I hope
for more than school uniforms
on the hangers, a King James
Bible on the mattress in the corner,
porn magazines on the dresser.
I hope to escape the mouths that sting,
the slamming of doors and the ritual
of tempers. I hope to hear more than
mosquitoes reciting lyrics in each
ear at night, my nieces and nephews
bawling out in the hall from fists,
the bickering over foolishness
and simple things. I hope to stop
tasting my father's liquor from
the dining room cabinet, to stop
stealing food for my sister, to stop
hiding in here. I hope for my knees
to bend and my prayers to make sense.

Rhea Manley

ELEGY

I am pouring
a little white rum and ting out
of my cup onto your lawn –
I don't drink much since we
broke up but I just
watched them put you
in the ground.

You are nowhere
I can see
it bothers me so
I close my eyes to find you:

it is Sunday
in *this* morning light
with your chicken sandwich
and Milo in my hands

I feel a bit like I am in a movie

we have been up all night
preparing
you are nervous and excited
I afflicted and exhausted
the sandwich I made is rubbish
but you look at me like I am your lucky charm

it is the first time I am watching you race
and I have skipped Father's Day lunch
to get sunstroke, meet your ex
and cheer you to third place

it is on *this* night
as I study you
as you sleep
that I realise
that I love you
and that we are doomed.

We still laugh for hours,
sit on the wall
drinking rum at
Dead End Beach.
I keep coming
to your races –
you never win.

We romanticise
that your failures
are about me
I am joking
but you say
I am a distraction
and besides
a girl like me
should have ambition.

I tell you that
that is foolishness
but you start to win.
Fuck it.
I was sick of scrubbing
your bathroom sink and
balaclava anyway.
I get a job.

Yet, I cannot help
but to miss
how your soap smelt
how smooth the skin
that covered the sparse
flesh over your bones
felt, and how
in the beginning
you would roll over
and hug me again
when you drifted off
in the night.

And I don't drink much
since we broke up but
I just watched them put you
in the ground so I am nursing
a white rum and ting turned

warm on your lawn
swaying to a dirge
we will never sing.

Jason Henry

SINCE

I've loved you
since the tide roared
and rose its tongue
to sweep me screaming
into its coarse mouth.

I loved you
when I was on the seabed
scratching the sand dunes
searching for the answers
and the escape.

I've loved you
ever since I realized
you lived underwater.

Jason Henry

[UNTITLED]

I bathed,
changed the sheets,
disinfected the countertops,
wiped clean the doorknobs,
ripped out the carpet,
filled the pool with bleach,
drained it,
burnt down the house,
burnt off my skin,
scraped myself off this damn
three-dimensional world
and cut my nose to spite my face

but I still smell you.

Britney Gabbidon

CHILD OF THE EARTH, DAUGHTER OF NONE

She is a child. She pins herself on clothes lines,
her shoulders indented by wooden pinches
and she watches the sun swallow and be swallowed
She is soaked by the rain at evening and dried crisp at midday
Her legs dangle,
her knees vulnerable to the will of the night wind
Her face is freckled by pollen,
her skin dusted
Tonight, she is a daughter
They unpin her left shoulder, then her right
She slumps, folds into a basket at her feet
She is adopted from nature
If only human hands were softer.

Teddense Thomas

A TRIP TO THE NATIONAL GALLERY

(Based on *Rasta Father and Child* by Rose Murray, 1975)

A black man captured
by a lens sits on his throne
in the back of his yard
with his princess on his lap.
Her hair like a mane
combed by nature,
brushed by the wind,
rubs against his cheek.

I stare for minutes wishing
that it was me caught in the frame.
To be a prince with my kinky hair
caressing the coarseness of his beard –
being sheltered by his locks,
and the pensive look in his face

Lisa Gaye Taylor

CHURCH HEATHEN

Dear Pastor, I come before you
And God to confess
That when I was to be in
Church on Sunday
I was at a soca fete

Took the money
That was to pay off
My student loan debt
And bought a carnival costume
So I could jump bacchanal
And get wet

Please Pastor forgive me
Two Sundays
When the choir was singing
I was humming
"I want a man
Come and ride mi riddim"

And when Sister Ivy
Turned her back
Started to soca butterfly
To a carnival track

Last night when I was
To kneel down and pray
All I could think was
How I want to rock Jouvert
And how I wanted to duck

Brother Joe with paint
Whe look every sister
Him is definitely no saint

Reverend for my sins
I am definitely not proud
But . . . I could swear a spot
Yu fine foot
In di crowd

Anyway, thank you Pastor for
Forgiving me
Your love and patience
Has set me free
Collection? Sorry Pastor
I am saving that fee
'Cause next year Powder Mas
Not missing me!!!

Sadé Young

OLD WOMAN

They took the photo without her knowing,
saturated with vibrant sepia tones.
It was an older style of photography that made
you nostalgic. As if the years had slipped by
and you too became ancient.

The woman was old,
not the elderly kind – chained to a bed,
not the kind that took to people fussing
about her. She was the kind that lived to
see the birth of a country. The kind that
had stories to tell and lessons to teach.
She was the kind that grew on yam and Irish potato.
The "It takes a village to raise a child" kind.

Sun blazing on her hunched back,
breasts sagging, arms crossed,
she makes the monthly journey to Spanish Town.
She walks by a wall older than herself,
whose red bricks have washed out over time.
her plaits sticking out from under the red tie head,
red sock – knee high,
red sneakers – one size too big,
she goes to confide in the obeah man, about the dead
husband she keeps seeing in her yard.

PLAYTHING

for Kimoya Ellis

sometimes
i see you
frolicking
in the downtown sun
givin laugh fi peas soup,
and my body is weak
with grief
folding over onto itself,
for death come too quick
to play dandy shandy
one over head,
two over head
cock up is a ten
tips is a out
and yuh out.
out.

Khadijah Chin

TAXI TALK

I am a passenger among women
in familiar perplexity
at the doggish nature of men.

"Den Aunty Shirley,"
a younger woman started,
"mi nuh undastan why she so shock seh ar man do it.
Den di wol a wi man nuh do it?
God bless you if you find a man
weh nuh hav one nex woman
pon di side."

And the women erupt
in chastising chants of
"Mm-hm" and "Amen" and
"Di dyam dutty dog dem!"

But the one designated preacher woman
incites us all to recall that
Woman was the first
to bring a devil into the marriage bed
and an astounded Adam
stuffed his mouth with fruit
to stifle his shame,
squealed to God
that the woman was to blame
and wove together leaves
to cover his iniquity
because her snake was stronger than his.

And since then, Man has whispered revenge
into the ears of his cronies,
established a pact
and told his crew that
ménage à trois
is the ideal stew to noose the neck of Woman,
that she may suffer too
and *that* is why there will always be trouble in paradise.

Christopher Allen

THE X FACTOR

When a man hugs another, we set our tongues
on fire, hang large stones around his neck,
pin scales and gills to his skin
and sink him into a deep sea of shame.

We whose pants sag, arses showing in the streets,
we who smoke and sip
from the same cigarette and cup
will put back our pot-covers of approval.

As if talent rubs off by touch and love for women
is burnt in male heat. We take back our thanks
as if he is no longer Jamaican.

Because he does not carry bible in back pocket,
a half-burnt *spliff* behind his ear,
rusty ratchet knife, the stench of rum on his breath.

For redemption he must paint his tongue red,
deepen voice, curl his face into hate.
Hawk bitter words from deep belly,
spit a bloody language:
go suck out yuh mada battybwoy.

Kiseon Thompson

UNDER EVERY STREET LIGHT WE SHINE

Dark and late we meet, after a day of pretending,
On the road down to home
Where it slopes to an end
And curves to a flat.

We hold hands in my mind and then never, then wholly, then never.
You touch me barely to pull shame out of your veins
But you walk close enough to feel my flesh relax, let you love me,
And now my legs are moving up and down through no will of my own.
I walk for you I feel your silence and you ask to feel my loud,
And I release the cymbals from under my neck
And the drums from my chest
And the organ from my hands
And the strings from my back
And you love that cacophony that drops from my waist.
And you respond by breathing the sheets to follow.
And the street lights are lighting our stage

– we perform.

Rohan Facey

SECRETS OF LAUNDRY DAY

On laundry day
She pulled secrets from his pockets:
a forgotten note, a crumpled photo of a woman
as breath-taking as the latest model of a luxury car,
loose threads; along with candy wrappers.

She saw also – lip prints on a snowy cotton shirt
she had pressed two mornings ago

Dirty linen
tumbled before her –
defying the power of detergents.

Delroy McGregor

THE GIRL ON THE BUS

The sun was ripe that morning
even in the biting breeze.
We descended past red awnings,
past green coconut trees.
My hands sweated in my pockets
soaking smooth plastic tickets,
my ribcage under assault at every
bump and jerk as we turned away
from potholes and patch work.

She was looking for a seat and sat
beside me. Her flat nose, fat red lips,
and brown skin held my attention
like a private plane zipping past
a truck on a highway.
Hello my name is Mary.
Nice to meet you Mary.

She was an aroma of spices: nutmeg,
cinnamon powder, vanilla. On the subject
of cornmeal porridge our voices lifted
above our classmates, the bus engine,
the wind in our ears, the BBC announcer
on the radio. We learnt we both liked
Saturday morning cartoons, stew peas
on a Sunday, sand on our skin at the beach,
the smell of mixed concrete.

That evening we sat at the back, sharing
earphones, mouthing the words
rude boy it is a pity, my hands
sweating in hers, my ribcage
under assault.

PART III

Khadijah Chin

WHAT THE POUI WEARS

1

The market lady on Heywood Street
sits with hips stretched
over a crush-cotton poui blossom skirt,
speckled with fish scales
and salt-sweat
and I forget where I am going,
stop to understand how
so much yellow can fit into one lifetime.

Fugacious blur, you bloom all at once
Fair flaxen snow of the tropics
Tawny teardrops mourning
the burning of free paper
Yellow bells beckoning the end of youth's beginning
You, an exclamation point at the opening of a sentence
You, a hallelujah in a steady chorus of amens
Trumpeting trove of winsome riot,
You get me every time.

2

Gap-toothed sheet
on the bed of lawn,
would it offend you if I said
you looked better from afar?

Artless, outstretched arms of cogwood,
begging will not make you pretty.
For now, when the lights are off,

you and your market woman are
retired to oblivion.

They who once wooed you with sweet-talk now pass you by, unseeing.
You know, they only loved you for your wares?

Khadijah Chin

CONTEMPLATING UGLI

Well, it's not *that ugly.*
There are uglier things.
But when you meld three
bumpy fruit bodies by force
you must spawn
something au fait with the grotesque.

But at least they're from the same family
– or maybe that makes it worse

like my brother who has an auntie and uncle,
who are his auntie and uncle on both sides

because Grandpa fell off the limb for Mama
but his staff kept guiding him into any other woman.

Generous man he was, always giving of himself!
So for every fruit the union bore,
Grandpa buried two seeds outside

and from the outskirts of that mother soil,
Daddy plucked a bloom to call his other
and Daddy, from that coupling
proffered my brother

and my brother's not that ugly either

but maybe that's not the same thing.

Trevann Hamilton

OLD CLOTHING STORE

She's the dilapidated building
On a corner in Downtown Kingston
Overlooking the harbour
Watching the sunlight dance off the waves
Creating ripples on her walls

Once having ladies walking in
In their Sunday best
Red lips and curly hair
Appropriately protected from the sun
Who isn't kind to skin like theirs

The paint is now peeling from the exterior in huge sheets in some places
The walls are wrinkled like the wizened old ladies' faces
Who often came in to retrieve their youth

Inside is now dark and dusty
People were once fighting to get in
And now they avoid the entrance like it's dangerous.

Trust them, don't open it up
Or you'll be deafened by the cries of the door
Howling to relieve the tension held in the hinges so long

The air inside is heavy and choking
Warning you not to venture more deeply inside
But the homeless
Broken and unfortunate
Have taken on the challenge
They have taken residence

But eventually they will be ushered away by the authorities
Or the unforgiving faculties in the building

She is uninhabitable
Condemned
But she has not crumbled to the ground
No, not yet.

Shannon Smith

PORTRAIT OF A DEPARTURE

Cool Manchester man, tall as baobab,
east Atlantic transplant
with grip and vigour in hand.
Sienna-hued tweed, draping arborescent form,
crowned in felt,
standing by water's edge, near empire's end
looking,

not at the road behind him
paved with destruction of his own laying
(As faulted as the rest they say
and so not unique in folly)
but rather ahead at the sea, ocean and steam liner
bringing the twice transplanted to mother country
to lif' up old iron, cinder block
and frock tail of all the London things gone

down. Joining Selvon's *boys* in West End dreaming
with white girls willing.
Gone to fight life and make a living
only to have it swept away in the pools
while the old fruit lef' out in the sun
drying to skin of bone

They say where baobab trees take root
the women bear good
and plenty too –

is true.

Nardia Reid

A BRANCH FROM THE PIMENTO TREE

As a child she used it to roll old bicycle tires
up and down the hill, racing to finish lines
stretched across the rotting light post, the starapple tree.

But as my mother she used it to deliver beatings,
to wait for tears and swollen skin,
for pleas never to do it again.

She used it to lift earth for renta yam,
dasheen, coco, irish potato,
to hook into the bellies of banana trees and drag them down,
to part vines, dig into earth to find her way home.

She shoved it under burnt pots to cook dinner,
eyes aflame for her children and their father;
who watched her turn grey and die.

We gathered at her wake, same pimento wood
was beating the sides of the drum
summoning us to chant and sing,
drink white rum, to twirl our hips under the moon.

Today men dig the earth with firm hands
waiting to bury her,
to bury her with the beatings, the fire, the drum,
with the ashes of a branch from the pimento tree.

Lauren Delapenha

AFTER THE HURRICANE

The day the awning swelled and broke right through,
she strayed out from the doorjamb to the yard.
I watched from under the still-dripping eaves
her slow survey of what had fallen with the leaves.
The storm so far had hit us hard.
She uttered not a word, but who

would care? She'd not the will nor weight
for words. The sky was all a scar, open wide.
The sun, a bloodless clot, had come undone.
Trailing sheets and socks, the clothesline knot
had come untied. The garden we could never
get to grow had burst to brutish spate

of desperate flowers, splintered leaves and wind-blown
glass. The rain had swelled the door ajar –
such gallantry, for whom? She was not
inclined to wander through the quiet rooms
and curtains bulging wet upon the sill,
sagging like a skein from broken bone,

and find her face pressed hard within the pane,
nor rummage through the earth's fresh-opened wound
and find her breath bound up in muted blooms
that crowd the mouths of utterance and drain,
entwined and stinking, sweet, fecund, profane
and learn that all we're not and all we are

will rot from lightning, thunder, wind, and rain.
No, she will stay here, eye to eye

with that unblinking round of nothing, round
which everything turns to nothing. Nothing sounds
a silence fiercer than the storm, but I
strain to hear it through the little breath

that never came. All the turning earth
is washed up here with the storm's afterbirth.
Here, there is no error and no oath,
just the entrails of our longing strewn
through roots that rot in the undergrowth,
through labyrinthine veins and our rough-hewn

proofs of being. We cannot name a ghost
we cannot see. Command the beast to crouch
and hold its breath behind the tree,
to sleep through storms and never wake,
and curse the ground that gaped to take
the child we found and lost, and lost, and lost.

But who knew that the sky swallows too?

And then the hour broke, irresolute,
like a name spoken underwater.
She turned herself towards me
and the whole earth turned with her too.
A soundless blue seeped through her eye,
like a hole in a bell.

And then I knew what to do.

I spoke your name and you were here, down
to strain our sorrow from the dew,
then up to make of the dawn a dream
and draw these waters back up through their stream
and further, to that source we've never seen
in another, higher yard we've never known.

Gail Hoad

MUSHROOMS ON A KINGSTON LAWN

I clean forgot
country folk call mushrooms
"duppy umbrella"
'til this damp morning
after days of rain
and browny-white buds
on stalks
among sharp green blades
they opened wide
round as old-time chalk dinner plates
undersides soft and lined
like pleated Granny skirts
to let out dusky ghosts
of yesterday

Demoy Lindo

A LITTLE BROWN SUGAR

The morning's cold perfume entrance all.
A blushing sun sticks its nose out for a sniff
the pipe flutes Mama's bucket
with a boom of water against the base,
filling to a high-pitched overflow.
She twists the tap to stop the performance.

I wake to fire tickling the bottom
of a blackened pot, the water inside giggling.

On the dining table, mint bush is growing
from my tea cup. Mama gloves her hand
with purple dish cloth and skilfully
streams hot water into my cup.

The sharp bitter needled my eyebrows together.
She smiles, adds some brown sugar
Takes my cup in hand and with a wave
of metal spoon sweet magic.

When I grow up, with longer hands,
and life gets bitter,
I will reach the second highest shelf
of Mama's breakfront, add a little brown sugar
to my sorrows, stir them into tea and sip.

Shannon Smith

SATURDAY SOUP

It is Saturday morning and I peel dasheen, turnips and cho-cho
in memory of the ones who taught me to be woman –
to take these tough and prickly provisions,
peel away their corruption,
cut them up against the gritted crease of my thumb
(no cutting board of progress today)
then simmer them down to something soft, aromatic and sweet.

Pimento seeds, thyme leaves, and token scotch bonnet
flotsam atop curry pumpkin tinged waves.
Dumplings, carefully folded to the centre,
pressed down by heel back of hand that they might hold.

Delicate soup water, where *scrapses* are elevated in stature,
where nothing of value is lost. Soup water distilling ousia
of chicken foot, cow skin or soup bone – ascending as sacred oil.
Soup water which restores what was robbed of the week.

And when has been found perfect flavour
we grin knowing tomorrow's will be better.
Then when it is through, we sit to a feast
fit for the salt of the earth.
A pity, it is, the passersby have all gone.

Rohan Facey

THE BROKEN STILL SING

A day ago –
I sat on my favourite limb
to coo a melody to sweeten the day,
and to flap my wings to the cadence of the wild,
wild wind.

But the hand of fate – knocked me,
flat-beaked on mean rocks, snapping my wings,
robbing me of flight adventures.

The wind became malevolent
and pushed me into a valley.
The rains came with glee
to laugh at my sudden plight;
and dust and debris flanked my existence.

But, a new song escaped my tremulous beak!
A new song – rich as inspired music that gives
way to goose pimples: The broken still sing –
A song of hope re-imagined, re-positioned.
The broken still sing.

Rohan Facey

SUDDEN FLIGHT

She flew away this morning
without murmuring. No farewell flap.
And no vision gave us a preview last night.

Her good deeds are left on the front porch
of our lives, and etched on our minds
like fine art.

The neighbours stood
in numbed groups. And the vicar begins to talk
about her in the past tense.

The house bears the absence
of early morning coffee, whispered prayers
and news on the telly.
The stove hums no tune again
And the utensils took on a deep silence.

Somehow, outside –
a persistent rain punctured the grey clouds.

Britney Gabbidon

STOMACH FIRES AND A BUTTERFLY

I watch as the boy places his hand on the stove top,
laughs,
tells me how it burns

Do you remember the butterfly?
How you crushed its yellow wings?

I remember how your lips had withered when you saw me . . .

You had two guns.
I could not decide which was more lethal, your hands or your tongue
Pierce both body and mind
Tell me,
which bleeds more?
which is better at hiding the wounds?

I see myself in the boy with the stomach fires.
When something grows too hot, you spit it out
But you stayed.
You hooked your name inside his mouth,
made him numb
Now, he has to press against stove tops to feel
something other than the
  ghost of your touch
and I,
I still feel like the butterfly.

Kiseon Thompson

HEALING IN THE GREENHOUSE

We grow, inside, on our own time, under the dark and late,
With the dim light that shows us ourselves possessed
By our own love smelling like the wild bush we are,
Creeping in the day,
Touched by white flies,
Our thorns un-contracting only at night
Where no one steps,
Making our piece of the cold air smell dark green and yellow.
Forgetting the sun,
We release fluid from our joints to move.
We are happy for dew,
We are completely gay.

We murmur and romp quietly
To keep our language from those who would speak it with
Our fruits in their mouths.
This language has no words.
And plants are the only ones I know to speak in unmoving energy.
It is being. Un-whole. Free. Growing. Still.

As the time passes, some of us hug ourselves and forget to let go.
Our roots nestle themselves to sleep
Because they are tired of holding us
And are wrinkled – being servants.

We too enjoy the night,
Hour after minute, whine after wine.
We own the colours and
Wear the perfume of each hue with pride.

We hum a spiritual to appreciate the sun, in which we wish to live,
Through the moon.
And this house you built in wood and rusty iron bars and black mesh is a sanctuary.

Rozan Levy

KINGSTON YARD

I should take more walks in the yard
because one day I'll leave home and realize
I didn't really get to know
the sweetsop tree that springs
from dirt and forms the letter *y*
with small tie-dye leaves,
some painted too brown and curling to sleep;
or this ackee tree whose racing partner
is a light post on the other side of the wall
spreading like the green bay tree in Psalms,
its red bunches hanging like art.

I've counted five eye-catching gardens
homes to colourful plants: lilies, Joseph's coat,
sweet roses, crown of thorns.
Flower pots too much to count
but I see scallions, leaf of life, lemongrass,
aloe vera spreading in its king-size bed.
Two mango trees, East Indian and Julie
this Kingston yard is fruitful home to many trees:
apple, lime, cherry, pomegranate, June plum,
jumbiline, bananas and plantains.
This yard bore me.

I should take more walks in the yard
to see colours of cars that honk their horns,
to observe the building blocks
now aged and green, bed rest for rusty steel,
to hear neighbours' chatter,
to see them and say good morning.
One day I will leave home and need these memories.

Kaleb D'Aguilar

THINKING ON THE GREEN I SEE IN TRANSIT

I.

Here, from London to Birmingham
travelling through on train
I see cabbage, lettuce, and sheep
The green is vast and never-ending
meeting a similar grey at the furthest point
We ride over this land
lost in the bleak terrain called England

Home, from Kingston to St Elizabeth
looking out my dad's pickup
I see carrot, tomato, cho-cho, jackfruit
orange, otahiti, banana
though we don't have fall,
we see colours all year round
with blue waters meeting yellow skies
and multiple shades of brown
bathing in the green.

Gail Hoad

WINDSONG

Gale-tossed ships aren't aimless things
Windblown leaves are sure
They follow the blasting breeze

Here I stand –

Feet on the beaten path
Eyes on the goal
Wind at my back
Hurricane in my head

| PART IV |

Khadijah Chin

FOR AFREAKA

She kneels, back arched,
spine aligned like rows of white men,
invaders, lining labourers,
waiting on deck.

What he calls "nature" and "making love"
to twist her nipples into a bright red,
not the roseate of Snow White's cheeks
or the scarlet of some Bible-coloured beast,
but the bruised and burning red of the blood of her impaled Christ,
a bloody Jesus she had only seen
sideways as the spirit boxed her to and fro
and when it was all over, she said,
Thank you, sah!
as he tossed her to the pit.

Later on, she would tell the children
that her neck was brusied from the laying on of gold
and her belly was distended from an allergy to gluten.
Shame still lining her palate, she would tell them:

Be always giving thanks
for someone had it harder than you.

Sit with legs crossed at the ankles,
hands set in the lap.

Be beautiful
and always say grace
and you must pray then this way:

Our Father who art in the White House
the Pentagon
Buckingham Palace
Save us, we pray, from the depths of despair
and make it rain on dem hoes
and di passa passa gyal dem

Tempt us not into freedom
and forgive us for even thinking about it.

For with you are sayings of everlasting life
and into your name, the lost runs and is given –

Remone Foster

OFF TO THE INDIES

Off to the Indies, I should go –
for in such pregnant lands come glory and gold.
My dearest Isabella, my Queen,
would it not pride you to be the first to grace its shores?
For even when our Portuguese brothers boast of Africa,
you will be obliged to call them mongrels and fools –
like wild animals they lack the logics of explorers,
and you took the route not easily taken,
you sailed west to reach the east.

Off to the Indies, I should go –
would the Church not approve?
Bells will ring and the thunderous hands of God will meet,
would it not please the bishops?
To root out evil in distant lands,
to rip the bosom of the heathens afar?
give me your blessings,
and I would give you all the glory,
for you did the unthinkable,
you sailed west to reach the east.

Off to the Indies, I should go –
give me ships, kind merchants,
and I will repay you with crude gold,
and do not torment and mock me,
like the misguided buffoons in England,
for they lack knowledge of what I know,
for I shall take the route not easily taken,
I shall sail west to reach the east.

Gail Hoad

TO TONI MORRISON – AUGUST 5, 2019

Miss Toni –
It funny
even now
after we know one another so long
how the things you say that show we come out of the one same big yard
still can surprise
and sweet we.

So right here
right now
we sing for you
as you fly back
like Solomon

A Rastafarian chant
A Revival hymn
A Church of God Pentecostal shout

No salt or grave or grief
shall hold your body down.

We going tell Mother Nanny
to wrap five thousand miles of rope make from blood wiss
round you waist
so that when you reach back
the ancestors will see
who
and where
you coming from
and count the sea-soaked knots you travelled
back home

We sending you with boil yam, okra, fresh fish
And cool coconut water
from the jelly man off Windward Road, Kingston, Jamaica,
just round the corner from Lorain, Ohio, USA

And you who write down
all the things
that sweet and sour we –

Like how we take bow leg in hungry baby for beauty
Why we bawl and say we dead before we live inna unfreedom
Beloved
Why when memory hurt
we want to rip it out
and forget
the backache of that chokecherry Tree –

You
Wings spread
wide as an eagle
Heart's anchor lifted
glide us eastward
across the green blue Atlantic
to
Home
Paradise.

Jovanté Anderson

REVIVAL

Madda di great stone, great stone of Babylon,
Madda di great stone got to move
Fire of hands come quivering like a quaking sun
come burning like judgment as it is written and written:
let this prayer quiet noises in the blood, echoes
in the bone, let the Spirit quicken tongues to tremble
truths that always swell the island like river water,
over ancient bodies that know the rawness of the earth
and taste the sleeping soil. I heard it sounding from
the angry mountains, shaking with the greenness
of a hundred feet that dig their heels and ask the question:
where are you, o God? O, come and cleanse this land
of death, reach the depths of sea to smite the sunken city
wipe the lust from their snickering skulls, and tear the
breast of Babylon out of our suckling mouths, o this we
ask of thee this day, to summon guns from newborn
hands and give them daily bread instead. Hide
us in the thickness of the trees, and come and see
these drums that dum-duku-dum-duku-dum-duku-dum
our penance into life, come and see these holy hips that
cut and twist and hold the wisdom stowed away on heaving ships.
This countryside is pregnant with this visitation, ushered in
by watchful white candles and weeping women in red and blue,
bodies dipping forward wrestling with eternity, shuffling
around tables of sacrifice, while this patient unbreathing ram
waits for them to find its newly spilled blood. Watch us
travelling through and through to sit at ancestral feet and
war with the spirits of iniquity that walk amongst us and
smile at nights when we close our eyes. We are dancing
out of this wretched place, tugged by those who came

before us to witness this timeless trial. And there we saw them,
trodding in twos, shackled and whipped and walking onto
their own vessels, commanded by River Mumma to sail into the storm
and flounder until their chests burst with the salt and the
excitement and excrement of fish. We stand in the fields,
stalks of cane sweet with sweat and swelling flesh and
them, begging ancestors not to set their cruel fingers ablaze.
Theirs is an endless sentence. And we all are baptized
in the flood of night, arms swaying, bodies spinning through
time and touching the tips of the curtain. And though we
strain to hear the whispers of tomorrow, we know
that it is good. And we taste the rain that pours on our
breaking shoulders and mingles with the white rum
that lingers on the air like a blessing. We stand waiting
for Madda Cynthia to command the wind of Pentecost
and blow upon the congregation. This here is a revival.

Kiseon Thompson

THE BACKSLIDER REMEMBERS BAPTISM

I remember when they filled
a pool with Jordan River
and lined us up to be swallowed
in our
                    white
linen and black skin.
Invisible cuffs, rattling,
orange with rust,
making a noise so familiar and
desperate –
like systolic waves crashing
from Sierra Leone to the Caribbean.
So convinced that these sinister
                    chains
were an act of God.

And oh, cold water climbed up my leg hairs,
froze me in place, and I let it.
Cold water reached up under my nuts,
picking them like an assault.
Cold water was another
promise from fire.
Cold water would wash away
life   and   death.

Old, bent bodies looked on us,
the newly captured,
cross over that great water.
Everybody watched our eyes close.
Everyone watched our lungs fill,
flailing.

I remember how we prayed away our bodies
to the lords:
come into us,
fill us with yourselves and expunge our
souls,
close our eyes and open our throats,
and dwell.

I vomited them out easy like exorcism.
It was *hot* water,
muddled with spit and frothing with sin.
I am hotter than any white ghost –
holy or not.

Khadijah Chin

A GLIMPSE OF GOD

You watch the world wake up
in slow motion,
illuminate
to a symphony of city birds
and the cock crows once.

Bodies shift to hug the opposite side of the bed,
heart singing in the slow steady hum
of a low steady drum beat
as you watch the world wake up,
stretch, then apply makeup.

Colour your blue face in shades of
vermillion, tawny and baby pink,
dislike it,
start fresh,
realize you are beautiful just the way you are,
leave yourself
in the plain raw naturality of daylight.

Somewhere, a baby is being born
as you watch the world wake up.

Push pause.
Listen to the sounds of the quiet.
Inhale a glimpse of your Maker.

Rojae Brown

EYE IT ALL BACK

I have not come to understand the weight
put on words sewn together like quilts.
Soft, soft they're strung to not misstate
but comfort, deep in instances of guilt.
I have sewn before, in bouts of affection
stacking and burning words to keep out the cold.
And yet, among those shawls of protection
I find the ruins, a maddening sadness doled.

It seems then that it is not my trade
to pen down the remedies of life
or to lip about an idle crusade.
There are razors in place of laugh.
Perhaps I'll try to eye it all back
To stare it down! in place of what I lack.

Lauren Delapenha

A BRIEF HISTORY OF ALTERNATING CURRENT

I live on 34th, a block away
from the hotel where Nikola Tesla died
alone in '43. Unremarkable,
except for principles like this, as he'd
agree: that things in close proximity
exchange their properties, as lovers do,
or lightning, separating strike from sound
to satisfy the ache that snaps both sky
and ground in fine excess of energy.

Born in an electric storm,
he'd often fling windows wide apart.
The midwife wrung her hands and said he'd grow
to be a child of darkness. No, replied
his mother, he would be a child of light.
Platitudes aside, were they not both right?
Photographers would shoot high voltage
stringing jagged through him without harm.
But, out of view, he'd sometimes see a blinding flash –
the internet has called this an affliction –
of terror alighting on every bright thing.

I lean my head against my window. I
can hear my fickle blood obey
its alternating currency, wired,
droning low, just like the June bug, years
ago, lamplight-drugged and lost inside
my coiling inner ear, spotting blood
on my shirt, trying to escape. As a child,
Tesla captured sixteen June bugs,

glued them to a tinsel windmill to make
a motor of their terror to escape.

Escape, too, the pigeon's sudden flight
who used the wings he spent his rent to heal
to fly away. He didn't pay. They cut his light.
He said he loved the bird as a man would love
a woman but he never loved a woman.
He left the window open and died the day she left,
when blood, denied its pathway through
his heart, reversed, and went the other way.

THE POETS

HELEN ZELL: YOUNG WRITERS' PRIZE FOR POETRY

Jovanté Anderson (2018 winner)
Lauren Delapenha (2018 winner)
Khadijah Chin (2019 winner)
Demoy Lindo (2020 winner)
Rojae Brown
Britney Gabbidon
Trevann Hamilton
Rozan Levy
Demoy Lindo
Teddense Thomas
Kiseon Thompson

EDWARD BAUGH PRIZE FOR POETRY

Delroy McGregor (2019 winner)
Romardo Lyons (2020 winner)
Remone Foster
Kacy Garvey
Jason Henry
Rhea Manley
Nardia Reid
Shannon Smith
Peta-Gaye Williams

LOUISE BENNETT-COVERLEY PRIZE FOR POETRY

Christopher Allen (2019 winner)
Sadé Young (2019 winner)
Gail Hoad (2020 winner)
Lisa Gaye Taylor

MICHAEL COOKE PRIZE FOR POETRY

Kaleb D'Aguilar (2019 winner)
Delano Frankson (2020 winner)
Rohan Facey